CHIVALRY

THE PATH OF LOVE

MEDIEVAL WISDOM

CHRONICLE BOOKS

SAN FRANCISCO

A Labyrinth Book

First published in the United States in 1994 by Chronicle Books.

Design by Meringue Management

The Little Wisdom Library–Medieval Wisdom was produced by Labyrinth
Publishing (UK) Ltd. Printed and bound in Italy.

Library of Congress Cataloging-in-Publication Data: Chivalry, Medieval Wisdom.

p. cm. (Medieval Wisdom) Includes bibliographical references.

ISBN 0–8118–0464–X

1. Chivalry—History. Chivalry—Miscellanea. 3. Knights and knighthood—History.

4. Civilization, Medieval. I. Chronicle Books (Firm) II. Series.

CR4513. C48   1994

394'.7 — dc20   93–29774
                                                   CIP

Distributed in Canada by Raincoast Books,

112 East Third Avenue, Vancouver, B.C. V5T 1C8

10 9 8 7 6 5 4 3 2 1

Chronicle Books

275 Fifth Street, San Francisco, CA 94103

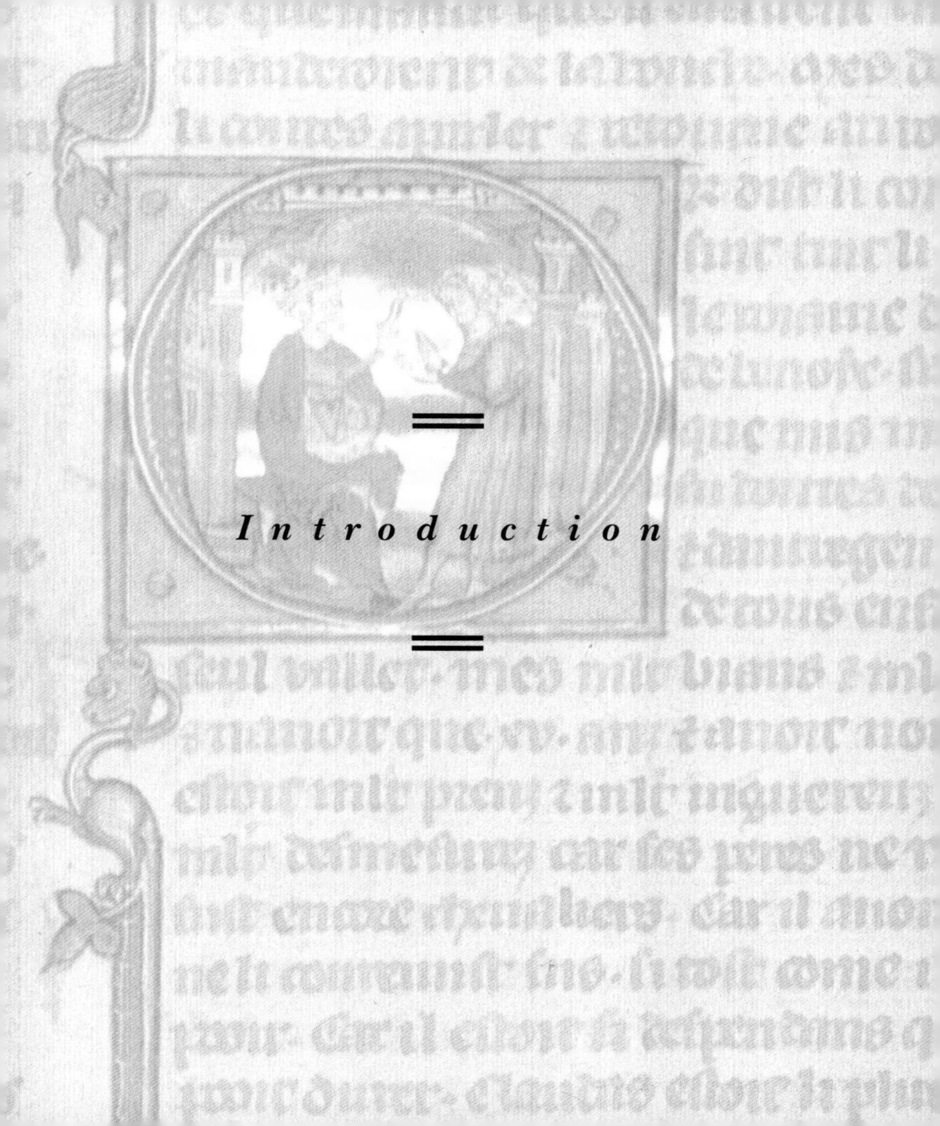

Introduction

This small book is a concise account of the medieval cult of chivalry. Chivalry was an ideal code of behavior for men at arms, especially for the nobility and for those who aspired to fame in the new European world of the twelfth and later centuries. It combined courage and steadfastness with personal honor, modest and unassuming manners and blazing loyalty to a cause, an ideal, or a lord, or— in the guise of courtly love— to a lady. Its scope might range from the conventions of the battlefield, through the manners of courts to the outpourings of intense, devoted passion expressed by the troubadour poets of France. From its beginnings, about 1100, to the end of the Middle Ages, and in the form of a code of gentlemanly manners for much longer, chivalry was a potent influence on European civilization.

The first focus of chivalry was the cult of courtly love, the idealized devotion of knights to their ladies and the deeds of heroism which they performed to gain their ladies' love. This is a theme which emerges in the songs and poems of the troubadour poets who wrote in the Provencal language between 1100 and 1300, and was taken up by the romancers of France and Germany. How far this kind of love existed outside the pages of the romances is questionable, but literature at least mirrored something of the realities of life in the castles of France, where real ladies like Marie, Countess of Champagne, or her mother Eleanor of Aquitaine, Queen of England, held court for perfect knights like William Marshal and poets like Chretien de Troyes.

William Marshal had made his career and reputation by deeds of arms under the patronage of the Count of Champagne, and thereby, became a friend and companion of kings and great feudal princes although he had no considerable possessions and a comparatively modest birth. Above all, he shone at the tournament, the great new jousting competition in which victory depended on horsemanship and a steady nerve in the saddle; the Counts of Champagne patronized the new sport, which earned them the

---

Page 4: Detail of an Italian tapestry showing a medieval jousting tournament. *Page 7:* Detail of the famous Unicorn tapestry.
Pages 8–9: A manuscript page from the *Romance of Lancelot du Lac.*
Opposite: Edward the Black Prince was known throughout Europe for his prowess in battles. *Following page:* A fully armored knight depicted in an English 15th C. tapestry.

---

gratitude of young knights like William Marshal by giving them essential training for war and an opportunity to make a name for themselves.

For these knights, chivalry was not simply a code of manners at court: it was an ideal of

empty rhetoric; it exercised a constant influence, through ideal models like St. Louis IX of France as Joinville described him: a king devoted to the crusade whose wars and government were exemplary in their chivalry.

liberality and restraint in the conduct of the countless wars of the age, which raised the dubbed or initiated warrior above the level of the savage, and made him an honored and worthy defender of the weak and the oppressed. The code was not just

After 1300, many more soldiers of fortune began to participate in war, as its material rewards, in the shape of wages, ransoms, pillage, and tribute, grew in value. The majority of these new recruits were not of noble origin, and many came from the poorer and more mountainous parts of Europe where the culture of chivalry had barely penetrated. Many moralists, therefore, strove to educate them in the code of chivalry. Popular works like the *Chroniques* of Froissart raised before them the example of paragons of chivalry like Edward the Black Prince or, closer perhaps to their own experience, that of the Bascot de Mauleon, a Gascon adventurer of humble origin whom Froissart nevertheless portrays as a chivalrous fighter.

At the same time, a kind of priesthood of chivalry grew up, through the heralds who arbitrated at tournaments and recorded deeds of arms on the battlefield. In their hands, the ideals of chivalry became a system of manners and conventions which slowly, though never entirely, became separated from the conduct of war. Heraldry, originally a method of distinguishing knights on the battlefield, became a mark of social standing, and Orders of Chivalry like the Golden Fleece and the Garter became decorations for the nobility and politicians. Chivalry and courtly love, however, never quite died. In the Renaissance and succeeding centuries, they were diluted and transformed to re-emerge as a code of gentlemanly conduct, the influence of which remained long after the Middle Ages. In literature and in life, chivalry made a permanent mark on western civilization.

Jeremy Catto
Fellow, Oriel College, Oxford

The Origins of Chivalry

Chivalry, as it tends to be portrayed by popular culture today, is a near-excessive gentlemanly courteousness. Its common caricature is represented by the man who, in the presence of a helpless and faint-hearted female, whips off his coat and lays it across a muddy stretch of ground so that the lady won't have to get her feet wet. But, in fact, this caricature is derived from the aspect of chivalry known as "courtly love," a later development of what had

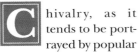

I tell you, food and wine and sleep are not so dear to me as the shouts of On, On! from both sides, and the neighing of steeds that have lost their riders, and the cries of Help, Help!; as the sight of men great and small ...

originated in the context of the battlefield, the relations between lord and vassal in feudal society, and a complex interplay of social forces including the Church. When the military codes of chivalry were elaborated to include the proper relations between men and women, some of the most powerful figures in this evolutionary development were, naturally, the women themselves. And, although in medieval times they did not call themselves feminists, they certainly represented a revolt

Previous page: A crusading knight as portrayed by the 15th C. painter Pinturicchio.

against centuries of oppression in which women had often been treated as instruments of the devil, unfortunately needed for the purpose of producing children but best kept firmly in their place.

> ... falling to the grass beyond the ditches; as the sight, at last, of the dead with the broken lance, pennant still fluttering, sticking out of the side.
>
> Bertran de Born, knight and troubadour

The origins of medieval chivalry, however, are to be found in a world inhabited exclusively by warlike and decidedly unchivalrous men. With the disintegration of the Roman Empire, Europe entered a period of chaos and almost constant warfare. The feudal system developed partly in response to this fact, as large landholders traded fiefs in return for military assistance in defending their holdings. The earliest armored "knights" differed in form more than substance from the nomadic "barbarians" who had hastened the fall of Rome. In fact, the early rituals of initiation into knighthood had much in common with the male rites of passage in the old tribal cultures, where a young warrior would pledge his loyalty to the tribal chief and where a failure of courage was cause for lifelong shame and humiliation. For both, the excitement of the battle was more important than the principles or land over which it was fought. And without the close-knit structure and discipline of the tribe, the vanquished arguably suffered more at the hands of anarchic feudal knights than they had in tribal warfare.

Apart from the reign of Charlemagne in France, and later of Otto in Germany, it can be said, without too much exaggeration, that the only stability and order to be had in the period often called the Dark Ages, from the sixth to the tenth centuries, was that offered by the monastic orders and the priesthood of the Church. There had been periodic attempts by the papacy in Rome to ally itself with

different monarchs, but these alliances were often short-lived. Both monarchs and popes claimed a divine right to rule, and their partnerships generally ended as soon as their ideas of what the rules should be diverged.

Nevertheless, the Church did manage, through these alliances—notably with Charlemagne and Otto—to insert itself more and more into secular affairs, blessing the marriages of the nobility, and sanctioning their claims to

Above: Charlemagne, here depicted with his consort, is crowned king and emperor of the Holy Roman Empire.
Opposite: The colored background is an enlarged detail from the medieval painting shown above.

> *The office of knight is to maintain and defend the holy faith catholic… and to honor and multiply the faith which has suffered in this world many travails, despites, and anguished death.*
>
> Book of the Order of Chivalry

authority and the authority of their descendants. In the rural areas, the clergy were called upon to bless knights and their weapons of battle, and eventually the ceremony of initiation into knighthood included a formally religious component.

Finally, motivated partly by dedication to Christian ideals and partly by self interest—the priests were themselves often landholders and knights—the clergy began to preach a set of chivalric principles, eventually known as Pax Dei, the Peace of God. The proper role of armies, they said, was to uphold the Christian faith, not to terrorize and rob peasants and reduce the landscape to ruins. It was a civilizing ideal, in comparison to mere bloodlust and greed. It was an ideal that in those times could come only from the clergy, not from the warriors themselves.

In November of 1095, when Pope Urban II declared the first of the Crusades, the ideal took hold in the very fabric of knighthood itself. Urban began by scolding his audience severely, saying they were no better than murderers and thieves, and reminding them that "the true soldiery of Christ does not rend asunder the sheepfold of the Redeemer." He exhorted them to fight for something higher than themselves, and more significant than booty.

In facing the dangers of recapturing Jerusalem from the Saracens, he urged, "May you deem it a beautiful thing to die for Christ in that city in which He died for us." Many historians believe that this marriage of faith to the fighting man of the Crusades, and the code of honorable conduct that grew out of it, was the real beginning of chivalry.

Above: The seal of the Knights Templar. *Opposite:* This romantic image of knighthood was a later development in medieval chivalry, and one more appropriate to times of peace.

At first however, perhaps to his dismay, Urban's call to the Crusades was taken up by an army of the poor, later to be called the People's Crusade. Consumed by an ignorant and fanatic enthusiasm, they marched off to slaughter Jews in Germany, ransack Hungary, and pillage Constantinople, before they finally met up with the Turks and were massacred themselves. The nobility followed shortly thereafter, in considerably more style and with less incidental brutality along the way. But the new ideals of chivalry, still in their infancy, exempted the knights from exercising any restraint in slaughtering the "infidels" at Antioch and Jerusalem. There, according to one Muslim historian, more than 70,000 were killed, including "a large number of imams and scholars, devout and ascetic men, far from their homelands, living in the pious seclusion of the holy places."

Perhaps the highest expression of the Christian military ideal of chivalry was found in the Knights of the Temple, or the Templars. Formally constituted in 1118, these Soldiers of Christ were a variation upon a more peaceful assemblage of both men and women, known as the Hospitallers. Before the conquest of Jerusalem by the Turks in 1071, the Hospitallers had lived a monastic life in that city, charged with the responsibility of looking after visiting western pilgrims. Banned during the period of Turkish rule, they were revived when Jerusalem was recaptured. Soon afterwards, the Hospitallers were provided

Left: A knight in armor of the Order of Our Savior's Passion is ready for battle. *Above:* This map of the Holy Land, *ca.* 1253, shows important landmarks.

with weapons as well as medical supplies, and the men of the order soon became the Brethren of St. John of Jerusalem, adding military defense to their caretaking duties. Although the Templars were considerably fiercer than their earlier counterparts, they retained the piety and devotion to higher purpose that had characterized the early Hospitallers. More than any others, these Templars embodied the principles of Christian chivalry laid out by Urban in his original call to the Crusades.

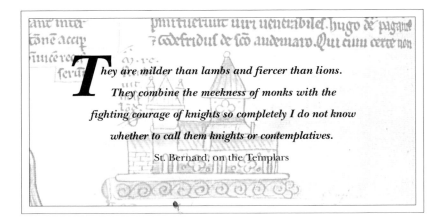

They are milder than lambs and fiercer than lions.
They combine the meekness of monks with the
fighting courage of knights so completely I do not know
whether to call them knights or contemplatives.

St. Bernard, on the Templars

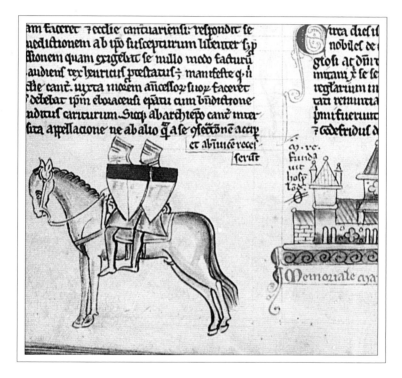

The Art of
Courtly Love

The majority of crusading knights waged war against the "infidels," plundered their cities, and went back home. But some of those who visited the Holy Land, either as crusaders or pilgrims, found themselves dangerously attracted to Eastern ways. They found in the Arab culture — both in Syria and in Moorish Spain, where many others fought— a refinement and beauty they had never seen before, an appreciation of the arts of poetry and song that had long been condemned as "pagan" by the clergy back home.

> In my lady's bower, none is more courteous and debonair; none, in the battlefield, is of greater power.
>
> Piere Vidal, troubadour

And, in their Arab opponents, they found a courage and gallantry that was often far more "chivalrous" than that exhibited by most of their fellow Christians.

While the Crusades gave birth to the Templars, on the one hand, they gave birth to the troubadours, on the other. These men, many unschooled but nevertheless talented in the minstrel arts of their pagan minstrel predecessors, returned to their homelands with their talents enriched by the "heresy" of the East. They found

Page 25: Two Templar Knights share a horse; this manuscript page also shows one of their hospitals in London.
Page 26: This illumination from a 14th C. version of *The Romance of the Rose* shows two lovers embracing. *Opposite:* the background used in the box depicts a medieval fortress, Kraks des Chevaliers, in Syria.

Sighing for my love I leave for Syria...A knight

does well by winning paradise and honor

And prizes and reputation and the love of his lady.

God is beleaguered in His own holy city.

Now we will succor Him who saved us

from Sin's dark prison

When He was nailed to the Cross that the

Turks have stolen from us.

Conon de Bethune (c.1150-1219),

Chanson de Croisade

a ready audience for their poetic tales, particularly in the Mediterranean lands which had long been under the influence of Muslim culture anyway. The very word "troubadour" derives from a combination of the Arabic word for music and song, with a suffix of the Spanish spoken in the lands where Muslims had long lived in relative peace, trading and sometimes intermarrying with their Christian neighbors. Within a very short time, the troubadours, by bringing the romance of the East to the long-suffering West, had begun to transform chivalry from its self-sacrificing Christian soldiery to the enduring tradition of legend and romantic idealism that it still represents in the popular imagination today.

William, Count of Poitou, was one of those who took up the cross and marched to Jerusalem shortly after the first Crusade. When he returned to his native land, something in him had changed. Whatever Christian piety or eagerness for battle had prompted him to join the Crusades in the first place had completely evaporated in the scorching deserts of the Middle East. And, as one of his

Opposite: Troubadours celebrate in song and dance the prowess of famous knights in battle. *Page 33:* The art of courtly love was initially deeply influenced by Persian devotional poetry, brought to Europe by Moorish invasions and subsequent settlements in the continent. This painting shows Persian poets.

contemporaries put it, he "wallowed as completely in the style of vice as though he believed that all things were governed by chance and not by Providence." He scandalized the local populace by abandoning his wife and taking the wife of another Count as his mistress. But the wicked and sacrilegious humor of his poetry won William an enthusiastic audience, whether he was advocating the setting up of an abbey of whores, or offering irreverent prayers—"May God grant that I live long enough to have my hands beneath her cloak,"

> Noble lady I ask of you
> To take me as your servitor;
> I'll serve you as I would my lord
> Whatever my reward shall be.
> Look, I am here at your command,
> You who are noble, gay and kind
> You are no bear or lion's whelp
> Who'll kill me if I yield to you.
>
> Bernart de Ventadour, troubadour

he pleads in one of his poems.

The sacrilege of William's poetry provoked laughter rather than outrage in the southern lands. The bawdiness and overt sexuality were a reflection of the changing times: with the energy of warfare directed towards foreign soil, a relative peace had come to much of Europe. Men spending less time on the battlefield turned their attentions to enjoying the pleasures of the company of women. William of Poitiers, veteran of the Crusade, who returned from Jerusalem bearing

ribald poetry and an eccentric life style, was the first troubadour.

Those who followed him were more refined than William, and generally more respectful of Christianity. But their songs and poetry drew on the same diverse and contradictory sources as those of the troubadour from Poitiers. To the Christian military chivalric ideal was added the Roman bawdiness of Ovid, who was enjoying a popular revival at the time. But Ovid's cynical advice for manipulating women was transformed into something more ingenuous, both by Arab influences and a lingering pagan spirit in the

This page: A page from the prologue to the illuminated manuscript of Chaucer's *The Canterbury Tales. Opposite:* Courtly love was directed to women of higher station, and knights experienced it as an elevating force.

European people. The Arab ideal of love, strongly influenced by the Persians, was more spiritual than sexual. The union of man and woman was seen by the Persians as a path to the state of transcendence, and union with the divine. The pagan cultures of northern Europe had once revered goddesses and bountiful maidens dispensing plenty, and the collective memory still held traces of the pagan mythology that paradise had been turned to wasteland when these women were raped at the hands of brutal and insensitive men. The religious aspects of this memory were expressed in the cult of the Virgin Mary; the secular aspects found a new home in the songs of the troubadours, trouvères, and minnesingers.

As the art of the troubadour took root, first in the Mediterranean cultures of southern Europe, spreading slowly to the more ascetic North, their songs and poetry wove all these diverse threads together. The result was embodied in legends such as *Lancelot* and the Grail legends that followed it. It was reflected in epic romances such as *Tristan and Isolde,* and *Orlando Furioso,* and in the works of Petrarch and Dante. Many of these romances carried a curious blend of aristocratic spirit, devotion to the Christian God, personal courage, near-deification of women, and a jealous, consuming, and often adulterous passion of love.

Eleanor and Marie

Undoubtedly one of the most powerful women of her time, Eleanor of Aquitaine was the granddaughter of William of

Above: A knight's encounter with a lady, from an illumination in the *Romance of Lancelot du Lac.*
Opposite: A troubadour entertains the ladies sitting around a fountain in a castle's garden.

Poitiers. Married at the age of fifteen to Louis VII, king of France, she ensured that the art of the troubadours flourished in the courts of her husband, his nobles, and her children. In the middle of the twelfth century, she left Louis to marry Henry II the King of England, to whom she brought both Aquitaine and her southern poets as a dowry.

> Were all the world mine
>
> From the sea to the Rhine
>
> I'd give it all away
>
> If England's Queen lay
>
> In my arms.
>
> Bernart de Ventadour,
> in honor of Eleanor

the story composed for her new husband by Robert Wace, who introduced the notion of the Round Table into the tale and solidified its association with the chivalric knightly virtues of the Crusades. She welcomed the troubadour Bernart de Ventadour (who, according to some stories, had been driven out of his previous home by a jealous husband) only to have him banished from the court by a jealous Henry. But in any case, Eleanor and her poets added the romance of the south to the Arthurian legends of England, and spread the new hybrid

In England, Eleanor may have met Geoffrey of Monmouth, who is credited with having produced the first written history of the legendary King Arthur, full of references to Celtic mythology. And she must have heard the variation on

through her children's courts in London, Rouen, and Troyes.

But Eleanor, it seems, was not a woman to settle down, and eventually she returned to Poitiers. There, she set up her own court, and completed the work of embroidering the Christian military code of chivalry with a code for romantic lovers. The transformation was cemented with the help of Eleanor's daughter, Marie of Champagne. When she joined her mother in Poitiers, Marie set about instituting the "courts of love." These were modeled precisely along the lines of the traditional feudal courts, where

> A true lover would rather be deprived of all his money and of everything that the human mind can imagine as indispensable to life rather than be without love, either hoped for or obtained.
>
> Andreas Cappellanus,
> *The Art of Courtly Love*

disputes between retainers had been settled by the powerful lord. In Marie's courts of love, however, discussion centered on disputes between lovers, and the disputes were settled by the assembled noblewomen under the direction of Eleanor and Marie.

It was Marie of Champagne who directed Chrétien de Troyes to write *Lancelot*. It was a project he abandoned before it was finished, some say because he objected to the implicit approval of the adulterous affair between Lancelot and Guinevere that Marie had directed. But the appeal of the legend was irresistible—later poets completed the story on Chrétien's behalf, adding their own cultural and moral ingredients. Some variations dwelt on such virtues as Christian chastity, others hinted at parallels to the transformative quest of the mystical alchemists. But all of them contained the enduring themes of love as a relentless fire within the human heart, and reverence for the female principle as the way to redemption and restoration of paradise on earth.

Eventually, Marie returned to her husband's court at Troyes, and there directed her chaplain, Andreas Capellanus, to memorialize the events of Poitiers in *The Art of Courtly Love*. This witty and irreverent guide to the chivalric codes of romantic love is a document that could almost be

Above: A Persian musician puts notes to poetry, an art later adopted by the troubadours.
Opposite: The background in the box is King Arthur's famous Round Table, today kept in the great hall at Winchester Castle, England.

*Their high feast was love, who gilded
all their joys. Love brought them as
homage the Round Table and all its company
a thousand times a day.
What better food could they have for body or soul?
Man was there with woman, and woman there with man.
What else should they be needing?
They had what they were meant to have.
They had reached the goal of their desire.*

Gottfried von Strassburg, *Tristan and Isolde*

Lancelot knew such joy, such pleasure the night long, that he could hardly bear the coming of day when he had to leave his lover's bed. Wrenching himself away was crucifixion. Torn with misery he bowed to her bed as if it were an altar, and left the room.

Chrétien de Troyes

contemporary, were it not for its very feudalistic dismissal of the capacity of peasants to appreciate love in any form. The document raises love to a kind of religion in itself, "the fountain and origin of all good things."

The Art of Courtly Love devotes many of its pages to teaching by example, with dialogues contrived to show the proper behavior between men and women of the differing feudal classes. These

echo many of the earlier democratic ideals of military chivalry, allowing that even those of lesser birth might gain the love of noble men and women if their character was worthy and their adherence to the ideals of chivalry was impeccable.

Many of the admonitions in Andreas' "textbook" clearly came from the women who directed its writing: "He who shines with the light of one love

Above: A medieval troubadour. *Opposite:* The background in the box is taken from the illuminated page of a Flemish Psalter, illustrating everyday scenes such as this one depicting the pleasures of the flesh.

can hardly think of embracing another woman," says one passage, "even a beautiful one." And, "nothing which a lover gets from his beloved is pleasing unless she gives it of her own free will." The question of free will, however, brought up a particularly thorny problem in terms of the Christian prohibition against adultery. "Love cannot exert its powers between two people who are married to each other," Andreas declares. "For lovers give each other everything freely, under no compulsion of necessity, but married people are duty bound to give in to each other's desires."

This adulterous theme, found here, and in so many of the romantic legends of the Middle Ages, may seem oddly out of place in a time when the Church was expanding and consolidating

Above: This intricately carved piece forms the back of a lady's mirror which would have been given as a token of love. *Opposite:* Cupid shot arrows into the hearts of knights and damsels who fell victim to love.

its power over the hearts and minds of the European people. But in a way, by condemning the pleasures of the flesh even in marriage, the Church itself had created the seeds of this rebellion. Medieval marriages, particularly among the nobility, were most often arranged affairs based on political expediency rather than mutual attraction. What were people to do with the undeniable fact that they took pleasure in sex? They dressed their desire in a cloak of romantic love, put its power in the hands of Cupid, or Venus, or some other force beyond their control, and insisted on giving love its rightful place in the chivalric codes of the day.

It is hard to say whether people actually acted on the adulterous impulses espoused by the poets and sanctified by the Courts of Love. But they certainly must have enjoyed the validity these legends and songs gave to their romantic fantasies, as opposed to the threatened eternal damnation offered by the Church. And, for those less inclined to adulterous fantasies, there were many other romances in which the

Church strictures were observed by denying the lovers any real opportunity to meet, or even by having them lie chastely together without succumbing to the temptations of the flesh.

The Art of Courtly Love provides an intimate glimpse into the romantic idealism of the times, from its list of appropriate gifts to a lady (a handkerchief, a wreath of gold or silver, a purse, a comb, a mirror, etc.) to its sampling of the pronouncements of the Courts of Love presided over by Eleanor and Marie. In one of these, a woman is chastised for trying to restrain a man from leaving her, despite the fact that she does not really love him. "It is considered very unseemly," says the judgment, "for a woman to seek to be loved and

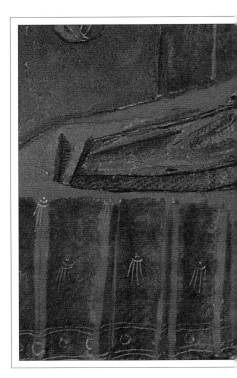

yet to refuse to love. It is silly for anybody disrespectfully to ask of others what she herself wholly refuses to give to others."

By the end of the twelfth century, the female descendants of the first troubadour had put women at the center of courtly life, and love on a throne modeled on the throne of God Himself. In doing so, they had changed the face of chivalry forever.

Previous pages: A 15th C. French rendition of Boccaccio's story of Troilus and Cressida, two famous medieval lovers. *This page:* A scene from the story of Troilus and Cressida. *Opposite:* The background in the box is taken from a painting of two troubadours.

Marriage is no real excuse for not loving.

— He who is not jealous cannot love.

— No one can be bound by a double love.

—It is well known that love is always increasing or decreasing.

—Boys do not love until they arrive at the age of maturity.

—No one should be deprived of love without the very best of reasons.

—When made public, love rarely endures.

—Every act of a lover ends in the thought of his beloved.

—Love can deny nothing to love.

—Nothing forbids one woman being loved by two men,
or one man by two women.

— Excerpts from the 31 Rules given by the King of Love, recorded in
The Art of Courtly Love by Andreas Capellanus

Chivalry
in the
Late Middle Ages

Not so very long after Marie of Aquitaine had directed her chaplain in the writing of *The Art of Courtly Love,* the Christian Crusaders turned their attentions away from Jerusalem and towards their fellow Christians back in the stubbornly heretical lands of Languedoc. These particular heretics called themselves the Cathars, the "pure ones." Their priesthood, the *perfecti,* were an ascetic and chaste group of both men and women who were renowned for their healing abilities, and enjoyed a great deal of popular support in opposition to the ever-corrupt southern clergy.

The particular heresy of the Cathars, or Albigensians, can only be deduced from records of those who opposed them, since they were preachers and activists more than publishers of written scriptures. It seems fairly certain, though, that they scoffed at the idea of an omnipotent God, and

pointed out that it seemed much more likely that the world was ruled by a constant struggle between good and evil. And evil, in the Cathar doctrine, was personified by the angry Jehovah of the Old Testament. Furthermore, it appears that they thought Jesus and his mother Mary were not living people, or at least certainly not divine, but just symbols of the good. To the Cathars, the Church of Rome, in its insistence on the trinity of Father, Son and Holy Ghost, and in its propagation of rituals to honor them, was blasphemous.

Pages 50-51: A joust conducted in the presence of Richard II in 1394. *Opposite:* Ivory engravings of jousting knights originally forming the borders of a medieval chess board. *This page:* Pope Pius II arrives in Ancona to launch a Crusade.

Pope Innocent III, after the failure of his emissaries to persuade the Cathars to change their ways, declared a crusade against them in 1208. The Albigensian Crusades dragged on for thirty-five bloody and ruinous years, killing hundreds of thousands of Catholics and Cathars alike. The southern birthplace of romantic chivalry was left in ruins. Furthermore, the early Christian ideal of military chivalry was losing its power. After the Albigensian Crusades, just a few more Crusades to the Holy Land were organized, all of which were ineffective. Nobles began to hire mercenaries to fight on their behalf, and these surrogates had little use for the chivalry of the earlier Soldiers of Christ, nor were they bound by the traditional ties between noble and vassal. Jerusalem had been in the hands of the Saracens since Saladin had retaken it in 1187, and just a century after the end of the Albigensian Crusades, the Templar Knights themselves–those original paragons of the Christian chivalric ideal–were accused of heresy. The charges against them remain clouded by the fact that they were brought by defectors,

> Be loyal of hands and mouth, and serve every man as best you may. Seek the fellowship of good men; hearken to their words and remember them. Be humble and courteous wherever you go, boasting not nor talking overmuch, neither be dumb altogether. Look ...

and were pursued by those whose own political and economic interests might have weighed more heavily than a strict concern for the truth. But the Templars had been unable, in the end, to hold on to any part of the Holy Land, and the privileges and power they enjoyed seemed no longer justified to those who might once have supported them. In 1312, they were officially suppressed by Pope Clement V. Many were burned at the stake.

Chivalry lived on through the late Middle Ages less as a code of love than as a code of behavior in a world of professional war. It was an aristocratic ideal, rarely achieved in practice among the crude and mercenary recruits to both sides in the Anglo-French "Hundred Years' War." Defined and codified to instill in them some sense of honor, it was expressed in elaborately staged jousts and tournaments and in the ceremonies of prestigious secular societies, like the Order of the Garter. The code of honorable conduct in war began to be transmuted into a code of manners which was open to satire. Chaucer's Knight in the

> ... to it that no lady or damsel be in reproach through your default, nor any woman of whatsoeer quality. And if you fall into company where men speak disworshipfully of any woman, show by gracious words that it pleaseth you not, and depart.
>
> *Le Petit Jehan de Saintre*

Canterbury Tales was a figure of parody, obsessed with amorous intrigue and the minutiae of courtly behavior. In Cervantes' *Don Quixote,* chivalry had become high farce.

In the later romances and the satires upon them, the concern for proper behavior among those of different rank often paralyzed those who were not sure who was properly authorized to speak first, or which of two

nobles should ride ahead of the other when entering a town. In some stories, the absurdities extended even to the kitchens, where the chief cook reigned over the proceedings from a high stool, a wooden spoon for a scepter. From this kitchen throne, he made sure that a hierarchy was preserved that, for example, placed a breadkeeper above a cook because of the association of bread with the body of Christ. In others, a duke might be shown presiding over his court from a lofty throne, high above an

These British stamp images depict Arthurian characters, bringing the romance of the legend to modern times.

assembly that was ludicrously deferential. According to one story, when the hair of a particular duke fell out because of disease, 500 nobles of his court immediately had their heads shaved in order to follow his example.

But the more ingenuous romances and epics of earlier times kept the highest ideals of chivalry alive in the popular literature, and those ideals continue to live today.

The message of chivalry is somehow irresistible, an ever-receding horizon of hope that survives all wars and other disasters humankind has suffered through the centuries. It is a message of nobility of purpose, of respect and compassion for others, and of courage in the face of danger. It is a message of the joyful union of man and woman, together not out of duty but of the freedom of the heart. It is the union of flesh and spirit, of human and divine—bridged by a path of love.

Following page: A square taken from a medieval chess board.

Barber, Richard. *The Reign of Chivalry.* Boydell, London, 1980.

Cappelanus, Andreas. *The Art of Courtly Love.* J. J. Parry, trans. *Records of Civilization.* Columbia University Press, New York, 1941.

Foss, Michael. *Chivalry.* Michael Joseph, London, 1975.

Harper, Christopher. *The Ideals and Practice of Medieval Knighthood.* Boydell, London, 1988.

Heer, Friedrich. *The Medieval World.* George Wiedenfeld & Nicholson, London, 1990.

Barber, Richard. *The Knight and Chivalry.* London: Longmans/ Sphere Books, 1974.

Contamine, Philippe. *War in the Middle Ages.* Michael Jones, trans. Oxford: Blackwell, 1984.

Duby, Georges. *The Chivalrous Society.* C. Postan, trans. London: Edward Arnold, 1977.

Froissart. *Chronicles.* G. Brereton, trans. London: Penguin Classics, 1968.

Gies, F. *The Knight in History.* New York: Harper and Row, 1984.

Joinville and Villehardouin. *Chronicles of the Crusades.* London: Penguin Classics, 1963.

Keen, Maurice. *Chivalry.* London: Yale University Press, 1984.

Lewis, C. S. *The Allegory of Love.* Oxford: Oxford University Press, 1936.

Every effort has been made to trace all present copyright holders of the material used in this book, whether companies or individuals. Any omission is unintentional, and we will be pleased to correct errors in future editions of this book.

Text acknowledgments:

pp. 16, 29, 54: Foss, Michael. *Chivalry.* Michael Joseph, London, 1975.

p. 19: *The Book of the Order of Chivalry.* Theatrum Obis Terrarum Ltd., Amsterdam, 1976.

p. 24: James, B. S., trans. *The Letters of St. Bernard of Clairvaux.* Society for Promoting Christian Knowledge, London, 1953.

pp. 32, 38: Jeanroy, A. *La poésie lyrique des troubadours.* Toulouse-Paris, Paris, 1934.

pp. 39, 49: Cappelanus, Andreas. *The Art of Courtly Love.* J. J. Parry, trans. *Records of Civilization.* University of Columbia Press, New York, 1941.

Picture acknowledgments:

Scala Istituto Fotografica; Pages: 4, 7, 52.
Bodleian Library; Pages: 8, 21, 22, 23, 24, 26, 33, 34, 35, 36, 40, 42, 46, 48.
National Trust; Page: 12.
Siena Duomo; Pages: 14, 53.
British Library; Pages: 18, 19, 37, 43, 49.
Public Record Office; Page: 20.
Heidelberg University Library; Page: 31.
Hampshire County Council; Page: 41.
Lambeth Palace Library; Page: 50.
Royal Mail; Pages: 56, 57.